# WILLIE MAYS

# Read all of the books in this exciting, action-packed biography series!

Sports Heroes
and *LEGENDS*™

# WILLIEMAYS

## by Matt Doeden

TFCB Twenty-First Century Books/Minneapolis

Twenty-First Century Books
A division of Lerner Publishing Group, Inc.
241 First Avenue North
Minneapolis, MN 55401 U.S.A.

Website address: www.lernerbooks.com

Front cover: © Bettmann/CORBIS.
Back cover: © Aaron Kohr/Shutterstock Images.

Library of Congress Cataloging-in-Publication Data

Doeden, Matt.
    Willie Mays / by Matt Doeden.
        p.   cm. — (Sports heroes and legends)
    Includes bibliographical references and index.
    ISBN 978–0–7613–5370–6 (lib. bdg. : alk. paper)
    1. Mays, Willie, 1931—Juvenile literature.  2. Baseball players—United States—Biography—Juvenile literature.  I. Title.
GV865.M38D64 2011
796.357092—dc22 [B]                                                      2010000892

Manufactured in the United States of America
1 — VI — 7/15/10

# Contents

# The Catch

**W**hen the New York Giants took the field for Game 1 of the 1954 World Series, they were decided underdogs to the powerful Cleveland Indians. But the Giants had one thing in their favor—they had center fielder Willie Mays. In just two full seasons of major-league play, the twenty-three-year-old Mays had already become one of the best players in baseball.

Mays had done it all for the Giants in 1954. He had won the National League (NL) batting title with his .345 average. He had slugged forty-one home runs and played his center-field position as well as anyone in the history of the game. Not bad for a player who had missed the entire 1953 season and most of the 1952 season while serving in the U.S. Army.

In that first World Series game, the score was tied 2–2 in the top half of the eighth inning. The Indians were rallying, with runners on first and second and just one out. New York relief pitcher Don Liddle came into the game to pitch to Cleveland slugger Vic Wertz.

Liddle's pitching style often caused batters to hit the ball on the ground. Knowing this, Willie played a shallow center field. He stood closer to the infield than usual. That way, if a ground ball came up the middle, he could prevent the runner at second base from scoring.

But Liddle hung a pitch in the upper part of the strike zone, and Wertz pounced. He drove a long fly ball to deep center field. It looked like a sure extra-base hit that would score one, and possibly both, runners.

Willie turned and sprinted back toward the center-field wall. He looked back at the ball once as he ran. Then, with his back to home plate, he caught the ball over his shoulder. Knowing the runners could tag up and advance once he'd made the catch, Willie turned and threw the ball, all in one fluid motion. It was a perfect throw to second base. The runner at second base managed to advance to third, but the man at first couldn't move up a base.

Players, coaches, fans, and reporters alike could barely believe what they'd seen. An over-the-shoulder catch was almost unheard of in baseball. To this day, the play is known simply as The Catch. However, many people—including Willie himself—believed the throw was even better than The Catch.

"This was the throw of a giant, the throw of a howitzer [cannon] made human," wrote one reporter.

The Giants got the third out without allowing a run. The score remained 2–2 after nine innings. In the tenth, Willie came up big again. In the top half of the inning, he made another great play in the field. Wertz smacked a hit into deep left-center field. The ball appeared headed for the wall. On the bounce, Willie made a stellar backhanded pick. He fired the ball to the infield, holding Wertz to a double. Once again, the Indians failed to score.

In the bottom half of the tenth, Willie walked and stole second base. He was on base when pinch hitter Dusty Rhodes hit a game-winning three-run home run to right field. The Giants had shocked the Indians with a 5–2 victory and went on to sweep the World Series. Without The Catch and Willie's other jaw-dropping plays, the win might not have happened.

Willie Mays always insisted that The Catch really wasn't anything special. But baseball fans see it differently. The Catch remains one of a handful of plays that stand out in baseball history. That play launched Willie Mays into superstardom.

Willie's career spanned twenty-two seasons and included 660 home runs—the fourth-highest total in major-league history. His career batting average was an impressive .302. He led the league in steals for three seasons and won twelve straight

Gold Glove Awards. He made the NL All-Star Team every year of his career. He was also baseball's first African American super-star. But when most baseball fans hear the name Willie Mays, The Catch is the one play that springs to mind.

# Chapter | One

# Young Willie

**W**illiam Howard Mays Jr. was born in the rural South. His hometown was Westfield, near Birmingham, Alabama. His parents, William Sr. and Anna Sattlewhite, were both just eighteen years old when Willie was born. Both parents were athletes. In his free time, William Sr. played outfield on a semi-pro baseball team. He earned the nickname Kitty-Kat because he was so quick on his feet. Willie's mother had been a track star in high school.

Willie was born May 6, 1931, during the Great Depression. Hard times gripped the United States. Willie's family had little money, but few people did at the time. Willie later said that his family was never poor. "I don't recall that we had any suffering," he said. "As far as I remember, my dad always had work."

William worked as a railroad porter. In this job, he assisted and carried bags for train passengers. The job frequently took

William out of town. When Willie was three, his parents divorced. His mother remarried and later bore eleven more children.

Young Willie lived with his father. But he stayed in touch with his mother and her other children, who were Willie's half brothers and half sisters. Willie's aunt Sarah and aunt Ernestine—his mother's younger sisters—took care of Willie when his dad was away working. Later, Willie's dad got a job at a steel mill. He was able to stay at home with his son. But Willie's aunts lived with them as well.

According to Willie's dad, Willie was walking at just six months—much younger than most babies. The elder Mays got his son to walk by having him chase a baseball.

When Willie was growing up, the South was racially seg-regated, or separated. White and black children went to different schools. Whites and blacks used different bathrooms and drank from different water fountains. Many whites viewed African Americans as inferior. Employers refused to hire African Americans for all but the lowest-level jobs. Government officials often wouldn't let them vote. Even sports teams were segregated in this era. William's semipro baseball team had only African American players. At the professional level, African Americans were not allowed in baseball's major leagues. They had to play in the all-black Negro Leagues.

The elder Mays tried to pass on his passion for sports to Willie. He took Willie to watch his semipro baseball games. Willie sat on the bench alongside the grown-up players. They called him Buckduck, or just Buck.

Sure enough, Willie was a natural athlete. He was fast, with his dad's catlike reflexes. Father and son spent countless hours playing catch. The elder Mays drilled his son on difficult plays. Willie often played in pickup games in the neighborhood. He played with white kids as well as blacks. The youngsters had a hard time understanding why professionals didn't do the same. "We thought nothing of [playing together]," Willie later wrote. "It was the grown-ups who got upset."

Willie loved baseball, but then, he loved to play almost any sport. At the all-black Fairfield Industrial High School, he starred in three sports—baseball, football, and basketball. At age fifteen, he joined his father's semipro team, while also playing high school baseball. On his father's team, he outhit and outran the grown men. The team paid Willie $100 a month, a lot of money for a youngster at the time. Getting paid to play baseball was "like getting paid to eat ice cream," Willie said.

## FALLING FOR FOOTBALL

Willie loved to watch sports almost as much as he loved to play them. Miles College near Willie's home had a football team. Because he couldn't afford a ticket, Willie would walk to the field, climb a nearby tree, and watch the games from there. Once, when he was twelve, Willie lost his balance and fell out of the tree. He broke his arm.

Willie wasn't the only one excited about making money at sports. His dad knew how hard it was to work at the steel mills. "Once you get in, you never get out," the elder Mays said about that life. He saw that sports might be a way out of a life of hard, low-paying labor for his son.

## DISHWASHER WILLIE

Outside of baseball, Willie's only job as a kid was as a dishwasher at a lunch counter. Willie didn't last even one day. Overwhelmed by the number of dishes that needed washing, he quit then and there. Willie knew then that sports had better pan out for him, because he couldn't imagine himself with a nine-to-five job.

Father and son played side by side. William Mays had been a center fielder, but he was slowing down with age. So he moved to the less demanding position of left field, and Willie took over at center. Soon, William decided to retire from the team for good.

Willie later recalled his father's last game in the league. Willie was showing off a bit, charging at fly balls in left-center field that normally would have been his dad's responsibility. But Willie was still just a kid, and he didn't stop to think until later that he should have given his dad one last day of glory.

Despite Willie's behavior in that game, William Mays was pleased with his son's talent. And the news from the major leagues was encouraging. In 1946, the Brooklyn Dodgers signed the leagues' first-ever African American player, Jackie Robinson. Robinson debuted with the Dodgers a year later. Despite harassment from racist fans and players, he had broken the color barrier in baseball. All at once, Willie and countless other black ballplayers had a brand-new opportunity.

"Robinson was important to all blacks," Willie later said. "To make it into the majors and to take all the name calling, he had to be something special. He had to take all this for years, not just for Jackie Robinson, but for the nation. Because all eyes were on Jackie at that particular time. We were pulling for him. When Jackie came in, I automatically became a Dodger fan."

## JACKIE ROBINSON

Jackie Robinson was born on January 31, 1919, in Cairo, Georgia. He grew up in California. He starred in football, basketball, track and field, baseball, and tennis, both in high school and at the University of California, Los Angeles (UCLA). Robinson went on to serve in the U.S. military during World War II (1939–1945).

In 1945, Robinson joined the Kansas City Monarchs of the Negro Leagues. The young infielder was impressive. Around this time, Branch Rickey, president and general manager of the Brooklyn Dodgers, decided to challenge baseball tradition. He wanted to add an African American player to his team. Robinson was the man he singled out.

Robinson signed a minor-league contract with the Dodgers. He made his major-league debut in 1947. He quickly found himself at the center of controversy. Many fans and players did not want a black man playing alongside white men in the big leagues.

Despite facing intense criticism and racial abuse, Robinson became a star for the Dodgers. He was named Rookie of the Year in 1947. He went on to play for ten major-league seasons, batting .311 with 137 home runs. He was elected to the Baseball Hall of Fame in 1962.

While still playing high school ball, Willie moved on to another semipro team, the Fairfield Gray Sox. There, his all-around athleticism caught the eye of Piper Davis. Davis was a friend of William's and the manager of the Birmingham Black Barons, a Negro League team.

Davis told Willie that playing high school and semipro ball was against the rules. Only amateurs—people who didn't get paid for sports—could play in high school. Willie would have to quit his high school team if he got caught. When Willie told Davis that he didn't care if he got caught, Davis made him an offer. "If you want to play ball for money, have your daddy call me," Davis told Willie.

Willie didn't need to be told twice. He ran home and waited for his father to get home from work. William called Davis, and within a few days, Willie was on the practice field with the Black Barons.

Davis might have been a family friend, but that didn't mean he'd go easy on the sixteen-year-old. Willie had extraordinary ability, but he didn't play like his own man. Instead, he imitated major leaguer Joe DiMaggio. He copied DiMaggio in everything he did, from his swing to the way he played the outfield. Davis told Willie that he had to get over his fascination with DiMaggio and play like Willie Mays.

Willie had a rough start. At practice, Willie stepped into the batter's box to show his new coach what he could do. The pitcher threw a wicked curveball over the plate. Willie flinched and fell down to the dirt. With just one pitch, Davis had found something Willie Mays couldn't do—hit a curveball. Davis told Willie to work on his skills and come back the following season.

## JOE DIMAGGIO

Willie's childhood hero was Joe DiMaggio, an outfielder for the New York Yankees. As a child, Willie pretended to be DiMaggio and modeled his game after the future Hall of Famer. He even told his friends to call him DiMag.

DiMaggio, nicknamed the Yankee Clipper, played for the Yankees from 1936 to 1951. (He missed the 1943, 1944, and 1945 seasons while serving in the U.S. Army.) In his thirteen-year career, he won three Most Valuable Player (MVP) awards, batted .325, and hit 361 home runs. DiMaggio is most famous for his record fifty-six-game hitting streak in the summer of 1941.

In the meantime, Willie headed back to high school. There, during the 1947–1948 school year, he played quarterback for the school's football team and led the basketball team in scoring. As Davis had warned, school officials had learned of his semipro ball playing and barred him from the school's baseball team. Willie knew that he had let down his high school team-mates. But he also believed that playing semipro ball and bring-ing in extra money for his family had been the right choice. He was prepared to pay the price.

# Chapter Two

# The Road to the Big Leagues

In the spring of 1948, as soon as school was done for the year, seventeen-year-old Willie Mays joined the Chattanooga Choo Choos. This team was part of an unofficial minor league for the Negro Leagues. Soon after the season started, one of the d' outfielders broke a leg. Piper Davis called Willie to take his place.

Willie didn't play his first two games with the Barons. Davis told him to sit on the bench and watch. Then, in the third game, Davis gave the youngster a shot. Some of the older players objected. They saw Willie as little more than a child—but nobody dared confront Davis about the decision. And Willie made sure his teammates knew he could play. He collected two hits in the game, a Barons' victory. It was the last time anyone ever questioned whether Willie Mays belonged.

Davis liked what he'd seen. He agreed to pay Willie $250 per month, with a $50 bonus every month he had a batting average over .300. At first, Willie played left field, but Davis knew he would be better suited to center field. "My center fielder [Norman Robinson] could out-run Willie, but he couldn't out-throw him," Davis said. "Nobody, and I mean nobody, ever saw anybody throw a ball from the outfield like [Willie], or get rid of it so fast."

When Robinson got hurt a few weeks later, Willie took over in center field. Opponents soon learned what Davis already knew: you ran on Willie at your own risk. His arm was strong and accurate, and word soon got around. If you tried to take an extra base on Willie Mays, he'd throw you out.

Willie had two years of school left, and William insisted that he continue his education. So Willie returned to high school in the fall, even though the baseball season wasn't over. He played for the Barons only on Sundays. But when the Black Barons won their division and advanced to the Negro League World Series, William made an exception to the Sundays-only rule. In the series, Willie and his teammates faced the Homestead Grays, one of the most successful teams in Negro League history.

Baseball historians don't have a lot of information about Willie's 1948 season with the Black Barons or about the 1948 Negro League World Series. In this era of racial segregation, journalists didn't pay much attention to the Negro Leagues.

They didn't archive box scores and stats the way they did with the major leagues. But historians do know that the Black Barons lost the series four games to one. In the only win for Birmingham, Willie hit a single in the ninth inning. The hit scored another runner, helping the Barons come back for a 4–3 victory.

Nobody knew at the time that this would be the last World Series in the history of the Negro Leagues. Since Jackie Robinson had broken the color barrier in the major leagues, the best black players were following in his footsteps. Spectators quickly lost interest in the Negro Leagues. One team after another had to close down operations.

Because Birmingham didn't have a major-league franchise to compete for fans' attention, the Barons stayed in business. They joined the Negro American League, which had ten teams. The 1949 season was more of the same for young Willie. He played full-time with the team during the summer and part-time while school was in session.

Major-league teams knew a lot of talented players were still playing in what was left of the Negro Leagues. They sent scouts to assess and recruit players. Willie did catch the attention of some scouts. But because he was still in high school, he was not eligible to play in the majors. So he continued playing with the Barons and learning from Davis.

In May 1950, Willie made his father proud by graduating from high school. Negro League baseball had continued to disintegrate as more and more black players joined major-league teams. Still, Willie was with the Barons to start the 1950 season. That spring, the New York Giants sent a scout named Eddie Montague to one of Birmingham's games. The Giants wanted Montague to report on another Barons player, first baseman Alonzo Perry. But it wasn't Perry who captured Montague's attention.

---

### THE END OF THE NEGRO LEAGUES

As Willie Mays and other black stars left for the major leagues, the Negro American League soon faded in importance. Within a few years, the level of play was barely that of the low minor leagues. The Negro American League finally folded in 1958, although independent all-black teams continued to play exhibition games until 1966.

---

"When I arrived in Birmingham . . . I had no inkling [knowledge] of Willie Mays," Montague later wrote. "But during batting and fielding practice my eyes almost popped out of my head when I saw [Willie] swing the bat with great speed and power, and with hands that had the quickness of a young Joe Louis [a boxer] throwing punches. . . . This was the greatest young ballplayer I had ever seen in my scouting career."

Montague met with Willie after the game. He knew he wanted to sign the youngster. He also knew that he needed to hurry, because he'd seen a scout from the Brooklyn Dodgers—the Giants' biggest rival—at the game. Montague called Willie at home. He agreed to pay Willie a $5,000 signing bonus and $250 per month. The Giants also paid the Barons $10,000 for the right to pull Willie from their roster.

Just like that, nineteen-year-old Willie Mays was on the road to the big leagues. But he didn't go directly to New York to play for the Giants. He would start in the team's minor-league system. The Giants could have sent him to one of their southern teams. But many southerners still objected to blacks and whites playing baseball together. The Giants knew that if Willie played in the South, he might have to endure abuse and harassment by white spectators.

The North was more racially tolerant than the South. So the Giants sent Willie to a northern team, the Class-B Trenton Giants in Trenton, New Jersey. Class B was the lowest level in the minor leagues. In terms of talent, it was a step down from the Negro Leagues. Stepping back to Class B was tough for Willie to accept, but he didn't have much choice in the matter.

Willie boarded a train for Hagerstown, Maryland, where the Trenton Giants were playing the Hagerstown Braves. It was a stressful time for the nineteen-year-old. He was all alone. He had left behind everything and everyone he'd ever known. But Willie got a warm reception from his teammates. Pitcher Ed Monahan was waiting for Willie when he got off the train in Maryland.

### THE SAY HEY KID

When Willie joined the Trenton Giants, he had a hard time remembering everyone's name. When he wanted to get another player's attention, he'd shout out "Say hey." People started calling him the Say Hey Kid. The nickname stayed with him for the rest of his career.

While the team may have welcomed Willie with open arms, not everyone did. Hagerstown is on the border between North and South. In 1950, it was a segregated city. Willie, the team's only African American player, wasn't even allowed to stay in the same hotel as his white teammates.

Some teammates were appalled at this treatment. So that night, five of them climbed a fire escape at Willie's hotel to knock on his window. They wanted to make sure Willie was okay. Three of them even spent the night in his room, sleeping on the floor. This gesture reassured Willie that no matter how much racism he might face, his teammates were with him. "I was so thankful," Willie later said. "I felt that those guys understood my problems. They knew that, hey, if something would happen [racial violence against Willie], I might have got hurt, or I would have hurt somebody, and then I wouldn't have had a career."

As expected, many of the fans were verbally abusive toward Willie. Willie would have loved to play well in the face of his critics, but he struggled. He went zero for three in his debut. Willie's coaches still liked what they saw, however. They chalked up his bad performance to the extra pressure he faced. They told the young outfielder to relax and just focus on making contact at the plate.

It was good advice. As the season progressed, Willie's talent soon shone through. He started getting hits. He was spectacular in the field as well. His minor-league opponents soon discovered the rocket arm that players and coaches in the Negro Leagues knew all about.

Willie settled into his new situation. In Trenton, he rented a room near the ballpark. He lived, ate, and breathed baseball. In what little spare time he had, he played pool and went to the movies. Willie was the youngest player on the team, and he was well liked. His teammates loved his enthusiasm. His stellar play only gave them more reason to like him.

Willie exceeded everyone's expectations in that first season. He played eighty-one games for Trenton in 1950 and posted a batting average of .353. He also had twenty doubles, eight triples, and four home runs for the year. In the field, he posted a league-high seventeen assists (an outfielder gets an assist by throwing out a base runner). With numbers like that, Willie was on the fast track to the big leagues.

The Giants weren't about to let Willie waste away in Class B in 1951. Minor-league players move up through the system as they perform well. The next logical step for Willie would have been Class A ball or even Class AA. But the Giants decided he was ready for an even bigger jump than that. He was ready for AAA ball—the highest level in the minors. The Giants assigned Willie to their AAA team, the Minneapolis Millers in Minnesota. Once again, the Giants chose to protect Willie from racism by sending him to a northern city.

To prepare for the season, Willie went to spring training in Sanford, Florida. For the first exhibition (practice) game, Leo Durocher, the New York Giants' manager, was on hand to watch the team's prospects. Durocher knew that the AAA players were the ones most likely to join his big-league club during the season. He wanted to see what they could do. But while he would watch everyone, Willie was the one he'd really come to see. "Hey kid, what are you going to show me today?" Durocher asked Willie.

Millers manager Tommy Heath started Willie in left field instead of center field, but that didn't stop Willie from making a big impression. In the first inning, Willie chased a long fly ball. Durocher saw how fast Willie could run. He told Heath to put him in center field instead of left field. Heath obliged. Willie continued to give Durocher a show that day. He threw out a couple of base runners from center field. He hit a long home run and a double. He even stole a base.

---

*"There was nothing [Willie] couldn't do. He played as well as anybody who ever played the game. He had no shortcomings. You knew in the clutch, he was always going to hit the ball hard. In the field, he was instinctive. He got a great jump on every ball."*
—DICK GROAT, 1960 NATIONAL LEAGUE BATTING CHAMPION

---

The rest of spring training went just as well. Heath called Willie in before the season began and gave him a big compliment. "We're taking you with us to Minneapolis," Heath said.

"But I kind of have the feeling that you're not going to spend the whole summer with us. I think it's only a matter of time before the Giants call you up."

Life in Minneapolis was an adjustment for Willie. In April, on the day of the Millers' first game, Willie woke up and looked out his window. It was snowing! It was only the second time that Willie had seen snow in his life. Willie decided that the team couldn't possibly play a baseball game in the snow, so he went back to bed. A little while later, his phone rang. Heath was on the other end, furious that Willie wasn't at the ballpark. The team had brought in a helicopter to blow the snow off the field, and the game was about to begin. Willie got a late start that day, but he finished strong. In his debut for the Millers, he hit a home run and a double and led the team to a victory.

Willie didn't stop hitting for the Millers. He was on fire. After thirty-five games, he had eight home runs and led the league with a gaudy .477 batting average. That meant he was getting a hit almost half the time he went to bat. In the minors as well as the big leagues, a .300 batting average is considered good. A .350 average is outstanding. Batting .400 is extremely rare. But .477? Unheard of! Opposing pitchers were scared to pitch to Willie, and with good reason.

Willie's fielding may have been even more impressive. In one game, an opposing player named Taft Wright hit a long fly ball to Willie in center field. Willie realized that the ball was going to bounce high off the wall, out of his reach. But he didn't give up. He dug his spikes into the wall and half climbed, half ran up the wall to make an incredible catch. Wright, meanwhile, ran to second base and refused to leave the field when the umpire called him out. Wright simply didn't believe that Willie could have caught the ball. But Willie was making believers of his teammates, his coaches, and the big-league club in New York.

Things were going well for Willie and the Millers but going badly for the Giants. Coming into the season, most experts had predicted that New York would win the NL pennant. But the team failed to live up to expectations. They lost their first eleven games. Through a little more than a month of play, they were 17–19 and in fifth place. Durocher, who in his playing days was known for his intensity, felt that his team was playing without any fire. They needed a spark, and he knew just what that spark should be—a brash, enthusiastic twenty-year-old who was demolishing AAA pitching like few had ever done.

On May 25, Willie and his teammates were in Sioux City, Iowa. On his day off, Willie found a movie theater. He was a huge movie fan and spent much of his free time taking in the latest films. Willie was enjoying a movie when suddenly the lights came up. Someone walked out onto the stage to make an announcement: "If Willie Mays is in the audience, would he please report immediately to his manager at the hotel."

That was a surprise to Willie. His mind raced. What was wrong? Had something happened to someone in his family? Was he in trouble? Heath quickly put Willie's fears to rest. The New York Giants had called, he told Willie. They wanted him to report to the big-league club right away.

Normally, any AAA player would jump at the chance to go to the majors. But Willie liked Minneapolis and his teammates. His first reaction was to say no. He wanted to stay with his team and with the fans who had so warmly embraced him. Heath even called Durocher and had Willie tell him so. Durocher was not amused. He gave Willie an earful. He made it clear in no uncertain terms that Willie was to head for New York and then to Philadelphia to meet the team that night.

Willie wasn't happy about it—and neither were the fans in Minneapolis—but the decision was made. At twenty years old, Willie Mays was headed to the major leagues.

# Chapter Three

# New Uniforms

**W**illie arrived in New York on May 25 and immediately reported to the Giants' office. He met with team owner Horace Stoneham and signed a contract that paid him $5,000 for the season. For a twenty-year-old in 1951, this was a tremendous amount of money. Willie would use his earnings not only to support himself but also to help his mother and half siblings back in Alabama.

As he was leaving the office, Willie tried to show Stoneham that he was confident. "I hope I can get in a few games, get a few chances to help [the team]," he told the Giants owner. Stoneham interrupted Willie, shocked by what the youngster had just said. "Get in a few games? Get a few chances to help? Don't you know you're starting tonight?"

That was Willie's first clue as to how much the Giants were counting on him. With that news, he got on a train to

Philadelphia, where the Giants were playing a series against the Phillies. He met Leo Durocher at his hotel. "Glad to see you son," the manager told him. "Glad you're hitting .477."

The Giants gave Willie the number 24. Like Stoneham, Durocher let Willie know that the team wouldn't be easing him into his new role. Not only would he be starting in center field, he'd also be hitting third in the batting order. That, more than anything, spoke volumes about expectations for Willie Mays. Managers typically put their best hitter in the number-three spot in the batting order.

### HOME AWAY FROM HOME

During his rookie season, the Giants arranged for Willie to live with David and Anna Goosby, a New York couple. Since Willie was so young, the team thought he'd be better off with a family than living on his own. With the Goosbys, Willie had home-cooked meals and people to help him deal with his newfound celebrity.

Whether Willie's arrival sparked the Giants is debatable. In his debut, he went zero for five at the plate. In the field, he ran into New York's right fielder, letting a fly ball drop for a hit. The only highlight of his first game may have been batting practice, when he launched several impressive blasts into the outfield seats. Still, despite the lack of production from their new center fielder, the Giants won the game 8–5. It became a familiar pattern in the series. Over three games, Willie went zero for twelve. But the Giants won the games anyway.

Back at their home field, the Polo Grounds in New York, the Giants next faced the Boston Braves. Willie had yet to get a hit in the big leagues. He stepped into the batter's box against future Hall of Fame pitcher Warren Spahn, one of the greats of the game. Spahn decided to start the rookie out with a fastball, but Willie was ready for it. With a mighty swing, Willie launched a rocket clear over the left-field roof for a home run. Willie's first big-league hit had been a memorable one. Durocher later said that he'd never seen a ball leave a park that fast.

Willie's struggles weren't over just yet, however. He didn't get another hit that game. He went zero for two the next day before leaving the game with leg cramps. When he returned, he stayed cold. At one point, he was one for twenty-five in his big-league career for a laughable .040 batting average. The pressure was getting to the twenty-one-year-old. In tears after one game, he told his manager, "I can't hit up here."

Willie was sure the Giants would demote him back to AAA ball, but Durocher had other ideas. He believed that Willie had the talent to be a star. He told Willie that as long as he was managing the Giants, Willie would be his center fielder.

The two men made some adjustments to Willie's swing. The changes worked. Willie went two for four the next night, kicking off a hot hitting streak. In late June, Willie belted a game-winning three-run homer in extra innings. He also pieced together a ten-game hitting streak (at least one hit in ten straight games). Willie's fame began to grow. A newspaper printed a photo of him playing stickball (a street version of baseball) with some neighborhood children. Giants fans saw Willie as a playful kid himself. His enthusiasm and love of the game were infectious.

---

*"It's always seemed to me that when the fans cheered [for me], I did better. I believe this is true of every ballplayer who's ever lived."*

—WILLIE MAYS

---

The team was enjoying success as well. They climbed from fifth to second place. By early August, the Giants trailed the Dodgers in the standings by 13.5 games. The deficit seemed almost impossible to overcome. But the team was hot, and that margin slowly shriveled.

When the Dodgers came to the Polo Grounds for a three-game series beginning on August 14, the Giants knew they had to be at their best. They won the first game of the series 4–2. In the second, the teams were tied at 1–1 in the eighth inning. The Dodgers had a runner at third base with one out. Brooklyn outfielder Carl Furillo hit a fly ball to right-center field. Willie darted toward the ball and caught it in a sprint. The runner on third headed home. Willie didn't have time to stop and prepare for a throw. He simply twisted in midair and whipped the ball toward home. The play was wild and reckless, but the throw was perfect. Giants catcher Wes Westrum caught the ball and tagged out the runner, who could barely believe the ball was there waiting for him. The next inning, Willie got a hit in a two-run rally that gave the Giants a critical win.

### LOSING HIS CAP

Giants fans loved the hustle and hard work Willie showed in the outfield. He quickly became famous for losing his baseball cap as he sprinted around the field. Later in life, Willie admitted that his cap didn't always fall off by accident. He knew the fans liked it, so he wore a cap one size too large so that it would come off easily.

Willie's amazing play was the highlight of the series—a three-game sweep for the Giants. The wins helped propel the team to a sixteen-game winning streak, the longest streak in the National League since 1935. By the middle of September, the Giants had pulled to within 5.5 games of the Dodgers. The deficit was still sizable, but the team had trimmed it by eight games in a little more than a month.

The Giants' winning ways continued. They won their final seven games of the season to finish in a tie with the Dodgers atop the National League. The two teams would play a three-game series to determine the NL champion. The winner would go to the World Series. Willie had finished the regular season with a .274 batting average and twenty home runs in 121 games. He was named the NL Rookie of the Year for his efforts.

In the playoff series, the Giants won the first game 3–1, but the Dodgers came back with a 10–0 victory in Game 2. The third game, held at the Polo Grounds, would be a winner-take-all affair. The two teams went on to treat baseball fans to one of the best and most famous games in major-league history. Brooklyn held an early 1–0 lead, but the Giants tied the game in the seventh inning. The Dodgers responded quickly, however, scoring three runs to take a 4–1 advantage.

The Giants were down to their final three outs. Their prospects looked dim. They started the bottom of the ninth with two singles, bringing the tying run to the plate. After a pop fly out, Whitey Lockman smashed a double to left field, scoring a run. The Giants then had runners at first and third with one out. New York's Bobby Thompson stepped to the plate, with Willie in the on-deck circle (due to hit next).

Willie was nervous. He knew the Dodgers had to make a choice. They could pitch to Thompson or they could intentionally walk him to load the bases. That would leave everything up to Willie, who had struggled late in the season and was just one for ten in the three-game playoff. He watched and prayed that he would not have to come to the plate and carry the team's fate on his shoulders, or worse that Durocher would call him back to the dugout and use a pinch hitter. His prayers were answered. The Dodgers elected to go after Thompson, and he hit the second pitch he saw into the left-field seats. The crowd erupted. Television announcer Russ Hodges shouted, "The Giants win the pennant! The Giants win the pennant!"

Willie and his teammates mobbed Thompson at home plate. Down 13.5 games at one point, the Giants had completed what may have been the greatest comeback in baseball history. The feat would later be dubbed The Miracle of Coogan's Bluff. (Coogan's Bluff was the area in New York that was home to the Polo Grounds.)

The Giants didn't have much time to celebrate. The next day, they opened the World Series against the powerful New York Yankees and Willie's childhood hero, Joe DiMaggio. Before Game 1, Willie was too shy to introduce himself to DiMaggio, although he did stare at the Yankee superstar. Finally, a photographer decided to snap a picture of the rookie Mays and the veteran DiMaggio. So Willie got the chance to talk to and pose with his hero, an experience he described as a dream come true. And if that wasn't good enough, the Giants won the game 5–1 to take a lead in the series.

The two teams split the next two games, leaving the Giants with a 2–1 series lead. They needed just two more victories to take the best-of-seven series. But the amazing end-of-season comeback, along with an emotional three-game playoff, had left the team drained. The powerful Yankees were too much for the Giants to handle. The Yankees won the next three games to claim the championship. Willie performed poorly at the plate in the series, with just four hits (all singles) in twenty-two at-bats.

Willie soon had more on his mind than baseball. That summer the United States had gone to war in the Asian nation of Korea. The U.S. government was drafting young men, or calling them to military service. After the 1951 season, Willie got the news: he'd been drafted into the army.

Willie tried to protest his drafting. His army pay would be much smaller than his salary from the Giants. He claimed that he needed that big baseball salary to support his mother, half siblings, and other family members, and therefore he should not have to serve. But the army denied his appeal. Willie had no choice. He had to join the army.

His service time was to begin in the late spring of 1952. Until then, Willie rejoined the Giants. He started the season with the team but struggled—no doubt distracted by his pending military service. In thirty-four games, he batted just .236, with only four home runs. His final game before joining the military was in Brooklyn. Normally, Dodger fans had no love for Giants players, but the Brooklyn crowd gave Willie a standing ovation. They appreciated the sacrifice he was about to make as a soldier. The gesture touched Willie.

Life in the service suited Willie fine, he discovered. He had no difficulty passing basic training. The army chose not to send Willie overseas to fight. Instead, it sent Private Mays to Camp Eustis, Florida. His assignment was to help physically train other recruits. He led workouts and helped new soldiers get into fighting shape.

Willie also played in baseball games with other players who'd been drafted, as well as army officers. The officers were proud to share a field with major-league players. Willie played two seasons of this "Army League" baseball, hitting .420 and .389, respectively. Those numbers didn't mean a lot, considering the mostly nonprofessional competition, but at least Willie was able to keep playing and keep his skills somewhat sharp.

## THE BASKET CATCH

One of Willie's army teammates had an unusual way of catching the ball. Instead of extending his glove, the player held it low, down near his body, as if catching the ball in a basket. Willie teased his teammate for the technique at first. But he soon discovered that a basket catch left him in better position to throw the ball immediately. He could get the ball from his glove and to the infield a fraction of a second faster that way. Willie soon became famous for the basket catch.

Leo Durocher kept in touch with Willie, even sending him money from time to time. After Willie broke his ankle stealing a base in an army game, Durocher scolded him. He shouldn't be playing so hard, Durocher said, and risking further injury. But whether it was semipro ball, the army, or the big leagues, Willie knew only one way to play—all out.

Meanwhile, the Giants sputtered without their center fielder. They had been in first place when Willie had left the team, but they struggled after that. Durocher and the team badly missed Willie's contributions on the field and his team spirit in the dugout. Any time a Giant outfielder missed a fly ball, the dugout rang out with the words "Willie woulda had it." The team finished in second place in 1952 but dropped to fifth place in 1953.

Willie's final months in the army were difficult. The Army League season was over. Willie had little to do until his discharge in March 1954. Worst of all, his mother died during childbirth, leaving him with eleven young half siblings to support. He grew increasingly bitter at being forced to serve. He couldn't wait to get out.

The Giants shared his eagerness. Durocher wanted his center fielder back.

# Chapter Four

# The Toast of New York

Willie rejoined the Giants at spring training before the 1954 season. His teammates couldn't wait to get the clubhouse favorite back. But they decided to play a joke on Willie. When he finally walked back into the Giants' clubhouse, everyone on the team ignored him. They treated him like a nobody—like a rookie whose name they didn't know. Willie was confused and soon grew angry. He stormed off to the batting cage to let out his frustration. He slammed a pitch over the fence before his teammates finally let him in on the joke. Players doubled over with laughter as they gave Willie the warm welcome he'd been expecting.

The Giants expected big things out of Willie in 1954, and he exceeded those expectations. In the season opener against the Dodgers, with the score at 3–3 in the sixth inning, Willie cranked a home run. It smashed into the front of the upper deck and gave New York a 4–3 victory.

The hit was a sign of things to come for Willie and the Giants that season. By the end of May, Willie had fourteen home runs and a batting average of .300. By the end of June, he had twenty-four homers. He was on a tremendous pace. People began to wonder if he could challenge the home-run record of Babe Ruth, who hit sixty dingers in 1927. Meanwhile, the team was enjoying success. The Giants and Dodgers were engaged in a hotly contested battle for first place, leaving the rest of the National League in the dust.

Willie was selected to play in the All-Star Game that July. Although he didn't start at center field, he did manage to go one for two in the game. He felt honored just to be there. Everything seemed to be going Willie's way. He was playing at an extremely high level, and the Giants had pulled into first place.

But shortly after the All-Star Game, Willie got some bad news. His aunt Sarah—the woman who had helped to raise him—had died. Losing both his mother and his aunt within several months of each other was a painful blow for the twenty-three-year-old. He was so crushed that he couldn't bear to go to the cemetery for the funeral.

Willie never let his heartache affect his play, however. Despite missing several games to be with his family, he was still on a pace to challenge Ruth's home-run record. While many fans in New York and elsewhere rooted him on, some didn't like the idea of an African American eclipsing the popular Babe Ruth. The combination of baseball intrigue and racial tension made an irresistible story for the media. Newspapers covered Willie's pursuit of the record with intense interest. *Time* magazine ran a cover story on Willie that July.

### WILLIE MAYS DAY

The Giants honored Willie in 1954 by holding Willie Mays Day on August 8. The team gave Willie a television, an air conditioner, and a plot of land in the New York suburbs. His teammates honored him with still more gifts.

Willie had thirty-six homers through ninety-nine games—about two-thirds of the season. But Durocher didn't like what he was seeing out of his young center fielder. He told Willie that he was trying too hard to hit home runs. Durocher wanted Willie to shorten his swing. If he swung with less power, he'd get more base hits, the manager argued. More hits would give the Giants a better chance to win.

Willie didn't care much about records, so he did what his manager asked. As expected, his batting average climbed and his home-run production fell off. He hit just five more homers the rest of the season. Meanwhile, he batted .379 over the final third of the season and finished the year at an impressive .345. That average was good enough to earn him the NL batting title in a close finish over teammate Don Mueller and Brooklyn's Duke Snider. After the 1954 season, Willie's play earned him the National League's MVP Award.

Willie's stellar performance led the Giants to a relatively easy NL pennant, with the Giants beating the Dodgers by five games. In his second full major-league season, Willie was headed to his second World Series. He'd performed poorly in the first one, however, and was determined not to let the pressure get to him again.

The Giants faced the Cleveland Indians in the series. The Indians had enjoyed a fantastic regular season, winning an American-League-record 111 games—14 more than the Giants had won. The Indians had a top pitching staff and were heavy favorites to win the series. But Willie stole the show in Game 1 with The Catch, and the Giants won in ten innings. "Willie Mays made that great catch and we were never the same," said Indians manager Al Lopez.

The Giants won Game 2 by a score of 3–1. Then the series moved to Cleveland. In Game 3, Willie's RBI (run-batted-in) single helped the Giants win. They took a 3–0 series lead. New

York finished off the sweep in Game 4. They took an early 7–0 lead and held on to win 7–4.

After the final out, Willie celebrated with his team. He later recalled that Durocher hugged him and continued to hug him on and off as the Giants partied on through the night. It was a dream season for Willie and the Giants. After just two full seasons, Willie Mays was the toast of New York and arguably the best player in baseball.

---

**❝**From the moment I first saw Willie, he was my boy. After all the fathers [mentors] I'd had watching over me in my career I had finally got me a son [someone to mentor].**❞**

—LEO DUROCHER

---

Willie spent a lot of time with his family, especially during winter. He traveled to Alabama to see his half siblings, and his father visited him in New York often. But with both Aunt Sarah and his mother gone, he found fewer reasons to return home. So in the winter of 1954–55, he signed up to play winter-league baseball in Puerto Rico, an island territory in the Caribbean Sea.

Modern superstars don't play winter ball. It's reserved for younger, developing players. But in the 1950s, professional baseball players didn't make huge sums of money. Willie played winter ball because it offered him a paycheck. After a well-publicized fight with a teammate, though, Willie vowed that he'd never return to winter ball. He'd keep his focus on the major leagues.

The Giants signed Willie to a $30,000 contract before the 1955 season. Coming off a World Series title, an MVP season, and a big raise, his life may have seemed perfect. But trouble was brewing in the franchise. Leo Durocher and Giants' owner Horace Stoneham were embroiled in a feud. Rumors swirled that Durocher would be leaving the team. This was a big concern to Willie, who liked and trusted Durocher. Willie cornered his manager and made Durocher promise not to quit during the 1955 season.

The controversy over Durocher seemed to affect the whole team. The Giants started slowly. Willie hit only three home runs in all of April. Meanwhile, the Dodgers were red hot, winning twenty-two of their first twenty-four games. The season had barely started and already the Giants found themselves in a deep hole.

A year earlier, Durocher had asked Willie to hit fewer home runs. In 1955, he did the opposite, telling Willie to swing for the fences. Willie did. He started banging out homers at an impressive pace. But his batting average suffered. Pitchers had discovered that they could pitch Willie outside (on the side of the strike zone farthest from the hitter) and get away with it. Willie entered one of his first deep slumps since coming to the big leagues. In mid-June, Durocher benched him for a game. "[Willie] hasn't been helping the club," Durocher told reporters. "He has been making bad throws, and running the bases the same way. He may need a rest."

The benching got Willie's attention. He snapped out of his slump and started hitting again. His average climbed, and he continued to hit balls out of the park. He even stole twenty-four bases—his highest total to that point.

The Giants didn't enjoy the same success, however. By July 1, they were 34–39. While the team did improve in the second half of the season, finishing 80–74, they were never in the pennant race. Willie's stats—a .319 batting average and fifty-one home runs—were the high points for Giants fans in an otherwise forgettable season.

Even worse for Willie, the feud between Stoneham and Durocher had not gone away. During the season, Durocher had announced that 1955 would be his last year as manager of the Giants.

Change was afoot in Willie's personal life as well. He was a very private person, preferring to keep his life outside baseball to himself. But sometime in 1955, he had met a woman named

Marghuerite Wendell and fallen in love. She was two years older than Willie and had twice before been married. She had a nine-year-old daughter, Billie.

Willie and Marghuerite decided to get married, and they did not want to wait. Maryland didn't require a waiting period before marriage, so in February 1956, the couple drove to that state to tie the knot. They moved into a home in Manhattan. But they didn't have a lot of time to celebrate. Just a week after the wedding, Willie had to report to spring training.

The Giants' new manager, Bill Rigney, was waiting. Rigney was no stranger to Willie. He had been Willie's teammate on the 1951 pennant-winning team. But that didn't mean he would be easy on Willie.

Leo Durocher had always treated Willie a little differently from the other players. Durocher even advised Rigney never to yell at Willie. But that wasn't the way Rigney planned to manage. He wouldn't give Willie special treatment. He made his point on the first day of spring training, tearing into Willie for a high throw.

Rigney wasted little time reshaping the Giants roster. He traded players such as Monte Irvin and Alvin Dark, bringing in a number of fresh faces. But the new combination of players was a disaster. Willie and his teammates floundered, mired in sixth place after almost a month of play.

May 6—Willie's twenty-fifth birthday—was a bright spot in an otherwise dismal season. Against the Saint Louis Cardinals, Willie stole five bases and scored the winning run in a 5–4 Giants victory. That game wasn't nearly enough to keep New York in the pennant race, however. Willie's hitting began to fall off, and the team kept losing games. Willie's trademark enthusiasm was fading. He wasn't having fun. In one game, Willie failed to run to first on a short pop fly. Rigney fined him $100 for his lack of hustle.

Willie was the first player in baseball history to hit thirty or more homers and steal thirty or more bases in a single season. He did it in 1956 and again in 1957.

Willie ended a long 1956 season with a .296 batting average, thirty-six homers, and a league-high forty stolen bases. The Giants had endured a terrible year, finishing 67–87, in sixth place. Reporters searched for reasons for Willie's decreased production. Some blamed Rigney's management style. Others pinned the blame on Marghuerite, saying she was a bad influence on Willie. The combination of a new manager, a losing team, and media criticism of his family left Willie feeling bitter about his life in baseball. At age twenty-five, Willie was no longer a kid. His honeymoon with the New York fans and media was over.

# Chapter | Five

## Going West

By the 1957 season, rumors about the future of the Giants were swirling. Attendance had decreased, and the team's finances were in trouble. People said Stoneham might move the team to California to start fresh. Giants fans and players were shocked. Willie took some comfort in the news that the Giants had traded for Jackie Robinson, one of his heroes. But Robinson decided to retire rather than join the Giants. The decision was yet another disappointment for Willie.

The 1957 season was every bit as miserable as 1956 had been. Once again, the Giants kept losing. Then, in August, the rumors about the team leaving New York became fact. Beginning in 1958, the Giants would play in San Francisco, California. Meanwhile, the Dodgers would move to Los Angeles, California. Instead of three New York teams, the city would have only one, the Yankees. New Yorkers were outraged.

For the season, Willie improved on his 1956 numbers, batting .333 with thirty-five home runs and a league-leading thirty-eight stolen bases. But to fans, the numbers were hollow. The move to San Francisco hung like a cloud over the team and its fans. The Giants finished the season 69–85, again in sixth place. Still, in his final at bat of the season, the fans gave Willie a standing ovation. And with that, his days as a New York Giant were over.

In 1957, Willie became the first player in major-league history to hit at least twenty home runs, twenty doubles, and twenty triples in a single season.

Willie and Marguerite headed to San Francisco just a few days after the 1957 season ended. They arranged to buy a house near Seals Stadium, the Giants' new home. The house was in an all-white area, however, and many neighbors objected to an African American family moving in. The house's builder relented to public pressure and decided not to sell Willie the house.

The decision hurt Willie and Marguerite deeply. It seemed that racism was alive and well in northern California. Even a former MVP and World Series hero wasn't exempt. The San Francisco newspapers got hold of the story and made it front-page news. The mayor of San Francisco was embarrassed by the neighborhood's racism. He even offered to let Willie and his family stay at his house.

Facing public criticism, the home builder once again changed his mind. Willie and Marghuerite got the house after all. But it was a bitter introduction to San Francisco—made even worse when someone threw a brick through the living room window of the new house. By contrast, a number of neighbors came to the Mays family and offered their support. But Willie had yet to play a game in San Francisco, and already he felt unwelcome.

The other Giants didn't feel much more welcome. The people of San Francisco didn't seem enthused to have them there. Rigney tried to build excitement by singing Willie's praises. He predicted that Willie would break Babe Ruth's single-season home-run record. He also said that Willie would hit .380 and drive in 150 runs. But Rigney's wild claims seemed to backfire. The people of San Francisco were unimpressed by such bragging.

Willie was ready to get back to baseball. He had a new $75,000 contract—a very nice salary for the era. In spring training, he met a batch of young, new teammates. He was shocked to realize that at age twenty-six, he was one of the most experienced players on the team. With so many unfamiliar faces, Willie admitted that even his manager, Bill Rigney, was starting to look like an old friend.

Willie was in high demand among major-league teams. The Saint Louis Cardinals reportedly offered Stoneham and the Giants $1 million for Willie. It was an almost unheard-of sum for a baseball player at the time.

The season started with a familiar foe in unfamiliar territory. Both the Giants and the Dodgers had relocated, and their rivalry had traveled west. When the two teams opened the season in San Francisco, they brought in the dawn of Major League Baseball in California. Willie and the Giants did their part in winning over the San Francisco fans by pummeling the Dodgers and their ace pitcher Don Drysdale in an 8–0 victory. Willie went 2–5 and drove in two runs.

This promising beginning carried over into the next month and a half. The Giants performed above all expectations. By June 1, they were 28–17 and in first place in the National League. Willie went all out every night. He knew that giving 100 percent was the best way to win over fans. He was batting over .400 and playing his usual spectacular defense.

---

*"What made Willie different was his desire. He played the game as if he was the only one out there. His eyes would light up. His energy would kick in, and he'd be ready to go. He played so hard, it inspired me to get out there every game.*"

—HALL OF FAMER ERNIE BANKS

---

Willie's enthusiasm was fueled by a rookie named Orlando Cepeda. Willie took the young first baseman under his wing. He also helped keep the emotional Cepeda in line. Once, when an enraged Cepeda threatened an opposing manager with a baseball bat, Willie darted in. He laid out the youngster with a full-fledged tackle. Willie proceeded to sit on Cepeda and pin him down until his rage passed. "[Willie] helped me every way a man can help another man," Cepeda later said. "He put points on my batting average. He taught me plays. He even kept me out of trouble."

Midway through the season, Willie seemed to have hit a wall. He went into a deep slump. He felt tired and worried that he might be sick. He spent two days in a hospital. Doctors found nothing physically wrong with him. He was just wearing himself out, they said. He needed to pace himself over a 154-game season.

The slump continued. His batting average dipped to .320 in August. Finally, Willie found his swing again. But his struggles had cost his team in the standings. The Giants slipped back to third place and couldn't get any higher. Willie finished the season strong and challenged for another batting title, but Philadelphia's Richie Ashburn beat him out. Willie's numbers on the year were good, despite the prolonged slump. He batted .347 and hit twenty-nine home runs, but this was a far cry from the sixty-one homers Rigney had predicted.

---

### No Love from the Hometown Fans

Willie's 1958 season was great statistically. He finished second in the NL MVP voting. But the San Francisco fans didn't seem to appreciate his efforts. The fans voted on the team's MVP and picked Cepeda over Mays. Willie reasoned that because Cepeda was a rookie, San Francisco fans viewed him as one of their own, while in some ways Willie still belonged to New York.

---

Rumors started to fly about Willie's personal life. Neighbors reported that Willie and Marghuerite argued frequently.

According to some, Willie physically abused his wife. Others said just the opposite—that she had attacked Willie.

Regardless of their fiery relationship, the couple wanted a child. So in January 1959, they adopted a son, Michael. Willie was smitten with the baby and was eager to be a part of his everyday life. Willie got a bit of extra time with little Michael that spring when he gashed his leg in a slide. He had to sit out much of spring training. The cut required thirty-five stitches and kept Willie at home for two weeks.

Willie was all business once the 1959 season began. Once again, the Giants played well. They were in the thick of the pennant race for most of the year, bouncing around between first and third place in the league. On July 30, the team took control of first place and held that position for a month and a half. In an August game, Willie broke a finger while sliding into a base. His numbers suffered a little because of the injury, but the team continued to win.

On September 17, the Giants held a two-game lead over the Dodgers. But then their season fell apart. The team lost seven of their final eight games, and the Dodgers claimed the pennant. For the season, Willie had hit .313 with thirty-four home runs. The numbers might have been higher if he hadn't broken his finger, but 1959 was still an excellent season for both Willie and the team, despite their late collapse.

Willie and his family moved back to New York after the 1959 season. The New York fans still adored Willie, and Marghuerite felt more comfortable there. New York became their permanent home, while Willie rented an apartment in San Francisco for the upcoming baseball season.

Willie and the Giants had plenty of reasons to feel good about the 1960 season. They had come close in 1959. Young players such as Cepeda (who had moved to the outfield) and first baseman Willie McCovey were developing into excellent hitters. The team also had a new home—Candlestick Park. The brand-new park was spacious and quickly became famous for its swirling winds—which played havoc with fly balls.

The Giants started out hot, winning eighteen of their first twenty-five games and taking hold of first place. But they couldn't maintain that pace. They started losing and falling in the standings. Their own fans even booed them. Stoneham responded by firing Rigney in late June. Willie was shocked to hear the news and even disappointed. For all their early troubles, Willie and Rigney had finally developed a good working relationship. Former Giants scout Tom Sheehan was named the team's interim (temporary) manager. He would finish off the 1960 season. Stoneham would search for a permanent replacement after the season.

The change didn't help the team. If anything, the Giants got worse. They finished the season 79–75, in fifth place. It was a bitter disappointment for a team that had entered the season with pennant hopes. Willie finished the year batting .319 with twenty-nine homers. He had not enjoyed his time under Sheehan and was eager to begin the next season with a new manager. He felt the need for a change.

# Chapter | Six

# Big Changes

**W**illie's marriage was in trouble. He and Marghuerite still weren't getting along, and Willie was unhappy in their New York home. Early in 1961, the couple separated. Willie moved into a San Francisco apartment as divorce proceedings began.

After years of Giants mediocrity, Willie was excited to be getting a new manager. The new man in charge was Alvin Dark—a former teammate of Willie's. Dark's new coaching staff included several other former Giants from the 1951 team. With so much change in his life, some familiar faces seemed to be exactly what Willie needed. For his part, Dark was thrilled to have Willie on his team. He wrote Willie a letter, saying that the chance to manage such a great player was a real privilege. That was quite a difference from Rigney's more reserved, indifferent approach.

Dark was less popular with the San Francisco fans and media. Many New York reporters still covered the team, and

Dark paid more attention to them than to the local media. Hoping to win back fans, Willie was more eager than ever to perform. But while the team started out well, Willie struggled. He later admitted that he might have been trying too hard. He was overswinging, trying to do too much on every pitch.

### WELCOME HOME

In 1961, the Giants traveled to New York to play an exhibition game against the Yankees. It was the first time Willie had played in New York since the Giants had moved to California. Willie didn't know what kind of a reception he'd get. After all, he'd been part of a team that had abandoned New York. And this was Yankee Stadium, not the Polo Grounds. But when the public-address announcer started to call out Willie's name, the crowd erupted. The noise was deafening. The moment touched Willie deeply. He later admitted to shedding a few tears as the crowd cheered.

The Giants improved under Dark's leadership. They spent much of the early part of the season in first place before fading back to third. Willie's power stroke returned. He belted forty home runs in 1961 and posted a .308 batting average. (Meanwhile, Yankee Roger Maris hit a record-breaking sixty-one that year.)

Willie hit his three-hundredth career home run on July 4, 1961, against the Chicago Cubs. He was only thirty years old—one of the youngest players in baseball history to reach that milestone.

Willie's baseball life was looking up again, but he was at a low in his personal life. He was lonely. He missed having a relationship with a woman. So Willie talked to one of his good friends, basketball player Wilt Chamberlain. Chamberlain was a notorious ladies' man. He gave Willie the phone number of Mae Louise Allen. Willie called Mae and tried to introduce himself. But she thought someone was playing a joke, pretending to be Willie Mays on the phone. She hung up on him. Willie called back later and convinced her that he was for real. The two set up a date. They hit it off immediately.

The 1962 season was magical for Willie and the Giants. They started out red hot, building a record of 40–15 through the first several months of the season. They were locked in a fierce battle for first place with the Dodgers. The two teams ran neck and neck atop the National League for most of the season. And the season was longer than ever before, because Major League Baseball had expanded its schedule from 154 games to 162.

Willie Mays grew up
in Westfield, Alabama.

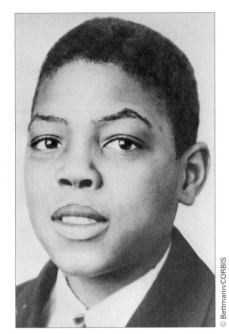

Willie *(right)* talks
with New York
Giants manager
Leo Durocher
during the 1951
season.

Willie poses at the Polo Grounds in New York City during his rookie season.

The Catch, made during the World Series opener on September 29, 1954, is one of Willie's most memorable moments.

More than forty-two thousand fans fill Candlestick Park for opening day in 1960.

Willie was known for his speed in the field and his amazing throwing arm. This photo was taken in 1962, during his days with the San Francisco Giants.

Willie Mays *(left, on base)* and Hank Aaron *(playing first base)* watch the pitch during a 1972 game. Mays and Aaron were rivals in the career home-run chase.

AP Photo

Willie smashes a hit during the 1973 season.

Willie *(right)* receives his Hall of Fame plaque from baseball commissioner Bowie Kuhn on August 5, 1979, at Cooperstown, New York.

Willie *(right)* exits *Air Force One* with President Barack Obama in Saint Louis, Missouri. They are on their way to the 2009 All-Star Game.

## MORE RIBS?

After one game in Milwaukee, Willie and Willie McCovey stopped for some ribs at a local restaurant. The food didn't sit well with Willie. In the middle of the night, he threw up in his hotel room. The trainer gave Willie a pill to help him sleep, but it did little good. Willie still felt terrible the next day and decided to sit out that day's game. But he attended batting practice and decided to take a few swings. He was pleasantly surprised. Although he felt ill, the ball flew off his bat. Willie crushed one ball after the next into the outfield stands. He decided then and there that no matter how bad he felt, he was going to play.

It was the right choice. Willie hit a long home run to center field in his first at bat. Then, two innings later, he socked another one. And on his third at bat, he hit one even farther. Willie hit a hard line drive in his fourth at bat, but Milwaukee's Hank Aaron caught it. Willie had one more chance. In the eighth inning, he stood in the batter's box facing relief pitcher Don McMahon. The right-handed pitcher threw Willie a fastball. Willie didn't miss it. The ball sailed more than 400 feet (122 meters) over the center field fence—home run number four! "How 'bout some more ribs?" McCovey joked when Willie came back to the dugout.

Dark resolved that Willie would get more days off. The star center fielder was thirty-one years old. He was no longer as durable as he'd once been. But with the pennant race so close, Dark's plan fell apart. He couldn't bear to have Willie sit out a game when each and every win was so valuable. So Willie kept on playing, though the games took their toll. One day he collapsed in the dugout and had to be rushed to the hospital. Doctors told him that he was suffering from exhaustion and to rest for three days. He missed three games, and the Giants lost all of them.

Few people blamed Dark for playing Willie so much. Willie was having one of the best seasons of his career. He was showing more power than ever before, racking up a career-high forty-nine homers and batting .304. He also made what he called the best fielding play of his career that year. Hank Aaron was on base when a teammate hit a long fly ball to deep center field. Aaron took off running, thinking Willie couldn't catch it. He was wrong. Willie tracked down the ball and made an outstanding catch. Aaron had rounded second base. He had to scramble all the way back to first before Willie could get the ball there. But instead of throwing to first base, Willie threw to second. Shortstop Jose Pagan caught the throw, confused.

Why hadn't Willie thrown to first? Willie pointed to the ground, and Pagan understood. He stepped on second base, and the umpire called Aaron out. Aaron had missed second base in his hurry to get back to first. The amazing part was that Willie's back had been turned at the time Aaron missed the bag. How did he know? Reporters grilled him after the game. Willie responded that he knew how Aaron ran. He had a feeling that Aaron had failed to touch the base. That play showed what an amazing instinct Willie had for the game.

By September 22, the Giants were four games behind the Dodgers. Only seven games remained in the season. Winning the pennant looked like a lost cause. But the Dodgers collapsed in the final week, and the Giants pulled into a first-place tie on the last day of the season. Willie hit a long home run in the final game to help secure the tie.

The Giants and Dodgers would settle the NL pennant with a three-game playoff. The situation reminded many of the 1951 season, when the two teams had played a three-game series for the pennant. Even Leo Durocher was there, though this time as a coach for the Dodgers. The first game would be in San Francisco, with the second and third (if needed) in Los Angeles. In Game 1, Willie hit two home runs in an 8–0 blowout. The first home run, a long bomb to right-center field, came off Sandy Koufax, the Dodgers' star pitcher.

The Giants appeared to have the pennant wrapped up in Game 2. They took a 5–0 lead early but couldn't hold on. The

Dodgers came back for a thrilling 8–7 victory, scoring the winning run in the bottom of the ninth. Game 3 would be a winner-take-all scenario for a trip to the World Series.

The game was played on October 3—eleven years to the day after Bobby Thompson had hit his famous home run in the 1951 playoff between the same two teams. Few were surprised that this Game 3 was another nail-biter. The Giants grabbed a 2–0 lead in the third inning. But over the next few innings, the Dodgers responded with four unanswered runs. The Giants came to the plate in the top of the ninth facing a two-run deficit. They had three outs to make something happen—or their season would be over. The Giants kept fighting, loading the bases with one out. Willie stepped to the plate. He knew that his team needed him more than ever. "I wanted to be up," Willie said. "I wanted [the pressure] to be on my shoulders ... I knew what had to be done."

On the first pitch, Willie hit a hard line drive straight up the middle. Dodger pitcher Ed Roebuck tried to catch the ball, but it tore the glove right off his hand. The ball never left the infield, but by the time the Dodgers defense reacted, all the runners were safe. The score stood at 4–3, and the bases were still loaded.

Cepeda tied the game with a sacrifice fly on the next at bat. The Dodgers seemed rattled. A wild pitch and two straight walks gave the Giants another run. They pushed the score to 6–4 when Willie scored on an error. That lead was plenty for the Giants. Willie caught the final out of the game. The Giants were headed back to the World Series!

---

*"Ted [Williams] and Willie were the toughest batters I ever faced. But I had a little success against Ted."*
—HALL OF FAME PITCHER WHITEY FORD ON HIS STRUGGLES GETTING WILLIE OUT

---

When the team's plane landed back in San Francisco, tens of thousands of fans cheered for Willie and the Giants. It had taken five years, but the San Francisco fans had finally embraced Willie Mays.

Once again, the celebration had to be cut short. The Yankees were waiting. The series opened in Candlestick Park, where the teams split the first two games, 6–2 Yankees and 2–0 Giants. Then it was back to New York for three games.

The Yankees won the third game 3–2, but San Francisco bounced back with a 7–3 victory to tie the series at two games apiece. Game 5 was tied 2–2 in the eighth inning, but New York's Tom Tresh hit a three-run homer in the bottom of the inning to give the Yankees another win, 5–3. The series was headed back to California. The Giants needed to win the final two games. But the teams had to wait—a huge storm was dumping rain on San Francisco. Game 6 was delayed for three days.

By the time the series finally resumed on October 15, the field was drenched. Willie had done little in the series at the plate, but he made his presence felt in the field. He frustrated Yankee hitters by tracking down balls that looked like extra-base hits. Willie also got a hit, stole a base, and scored a run in a 5–2 win for the Giants.

With the series tied 3–3, Game 7 would determine the World Series champion. Almost forty-four thousand excited baseball fans packed into Candlestick for the final game. They saw a great pitchers' duel. San Francisco's Jack Stanford and New York's Ralph Terry were both sharp, stifling opposing hitters. Stanford allowed only one run in the contest.

But Willie and the Giants hitters couldn't give their pitcher any support. Trailing 1–0 in the bottom of the ninth, the Giants found themselves with their backs to the wall. Matty Alou led off the inning with a bunt single, but the next two Giants hitters struck out.

Willie stepped to the plate with Alou on first and two outs. Terry threw a pitch to the outer part of the strike zone. Willie pounced. The ball soared over the first baseman's head and toward the right-field corner. Normally, the ball would have zipped through and given Willie a triple to tie the game. But because the field was so wet, the ball quickly lost speed. The right fielder held Willie to a double. Even more important, Alou was unable to score on the play.

Willie McCovey came to the plate next. He hit a hard line drive, but second baseman Bobby Richardson caught the ball for the final out of the game—and the season. The Giants had lost 1–0. They had to watch the Yankees celebrate on the wet Candlestick field.

Despite the loss, Willie and the Giants had had a great season. Willie had batted .304, with a league-leading forty-nine homers, and had finished second in the NL MVP voting. The long season, stressful World Series, and changes in his personal life had taken a toll on Willie, however. After the season, he checked himself into a hospital with exhaustion.

By this time, Willie was having money problems. Despite his high salary, he was building up debt. He had to pay for two homes—his own and his ex-wife's. He loved to wear expensive clothes, which contributed to his financial problems. Willie often traveled to New York to see his three-year-old son, but the visits were shorter than he would have liked. On the bright side, Willie's father moved to San Francisco to be with his son.

Before the 1963 season, the Yankees rewarded Mickey Mantle, their star outfielder, with a $100,000 contract. Horace

Willie loved to wear nice clothing. He was always sharply dressed, with his suits neatly pressed. Reporters joked that Willie cringed at the sight of even a wrinkle.

Stoneham didn't want to be outdone, and he knew that Willie needed money. So he upstaged the Yankees by giving Willie a contract worth $105,000.

Willie didn't live up to the big salary early in the season. He struggled, hitting under .300 by the end of May and slugging just seven home runs. Despite the slow start, thirty-two-year-old Willie was once again named to the NL All-Star Team. The All-Star Game proved to be one of the highlights of his 1963 season. He drove in two runs, scored two more, and stole two bases in the game. The National League won the game 5–3, and Willie was named All-Star MVP. Another highlight came on August 27, when Willie hit the four-hundredth home run of his career.

Willie's production had improved after his slow start, but once again the strain of a long season was getting to him. In September, while standing in the batter's box, he was overcome with dizziness. He needed help just to get off the field. He missed three games, once again with exhaustion. His absence ended the Giants' faint pennant hopes. The team finished 88–74, in third place. For the season, Willie batted .314, with thirty-eight home runs.

# Chapter Seven

# Chasing History

**W**hen the 1964 season started, Willie was closing in on his thirty-third birthday. He had a career total 406 home runs. Fans wondered whether he could challenge Mel Ott's NL home-run record of 511 or even Babe Ruth's major-league record of 714.

Willie's charge up baseball's career-home-run list continued that summer. He started the season on a hot streak, batting a jaw-dropping .497 after a month of play. That included a twenty-game hitting streak stretching from late April to early May. Age didn't seem to slow him down a bit as he cranked out forty-seven home runs in 1964. His average dipped a little, however, ending at .296—the first sub-.300 season he'd had since 1956. The Giants held on to first place as late as July 20 before fading and finishing fourth in the National League.

The early 1960s were critical years for the United States. The civil rights movement was in full force. In the South, African

Americans and their white supporters staged protests for voting rights, equal employment opportunities, and desegregation of schools and other public places. Against this backdrop of change and unrest, Jackie Robinson wrote a book about baseball and race.

The book included an interview with Alvin Dark, and many of Dark's statements sounded racist. He said that desegregation was happening too fast. He said that before the civil rights movement, whites in the South had taken care of blacks, as if African Americans were children who needed watching. And the controversy didn't end there. In his book, Robinson called out Willie for failing to use his fame and popularity to speak out about civil rights. Robinson accused Willie of forgetting his roots in a poor black neighborhood. He took shots at Willie's wealth and lavish lifestyle.

The uproar over the book and over Dark's comments was immediate. San Francisco reporters criticized Dark. Stoneham was furious with his manager. There was talk of revolt among the minority players on the Giants, which by then included many Latin Americans as well as African Americans. The black and Latino players gathered for a meeting in Willie's hotel room to discuss the situation. But Willie stood up for his manager. He said that he did not hold Dark's comments as a sign of racism.

Fearing serious backlash, Dark tried to quiet the controversy. He decided to make a symbolic statement. He asked Willie to serve as team captain. This was basically an honorary role as leader of the clubhouse. But no African American player had ever been named a team captain before. Many people said that white players wouldn't follow a black captain. But Dark said that Willie deserved the honor and that it was long overdue. Some people questioned Dark's motivation in making the move. But Willie embraced the role. He believed his manager when Dark said the job was based on merit, not on public relations.

Dark got himself in trouble again later in the season. He told a newspaper reporter, "We have trouble because we have so many Spanish-speaking and Negro players on the team. They are just not able to compete with the white ball player when it comes to mental alertness." Worse still for Willie, Dark pointed to Willie's promotion as team captain as a way to show that he wasn't a racist. Dark's act seemed to have been a public relations move after all. Willie could no longer stand up for his manager in the matter. Dark had said too much.

Predictably, 1964 was Dark's last season as the Giants' manager. Stoneham fired him and hired Herman Franks as his replacement for 1965. Franks was a popular choice. He'd worked with many of the players as a coach, and he spoke Spanish, which boosted his connection with the Latino players. His hiring helped ease a lot of the tensions in the clubhouse heading into the 1965 season. Stoneham had even asked Willie his opinion of Franks before making the hire. And Franks appreciated Willie, keeping him as captain and even expanding his duties. In many ways, Willie was like an assistant manager to Franks.

The 1965 season would be one of Willie's finest, despite a serious injury that he kept secret. Early in the season, he slipped and tore muscles in his shoulder and leg. The leg injury was minor, but the shoulder was a problem. Willie was famous for his rocket arm, but the injury robbed him of his strength. Willie used a bit of deception, which he learned from his hero Joe DiMaggio, to fool opposing players. Before some games, he'd uncork one long, hard throw, making sure the opposing team saw him do it. With the one throw, his arm was shot. But the other team didn't know that, so they wouldn't test him on the base paths.

That wasn't the end to Willie's injuries. In June, he pulled a groin muscle and was noticeably hobbled. Franks tried moving him to left field and right field—less demanding defensive positions. A few days later, the injury got worse. Willie collided with the catcher violently as he slid safely into home plate. He bruised his hip badly and had to go to the hospital. (The catcher had to be carried off on a stretcher.) The opposing manager,

Gene Mauch, spoke about the play after the game. "[Willie] comes into home four feet [1.2 m] in the air, kicks my catcher in the face, and still manages to touch home plate. He'll limp into the Hall of Fame."

## An Ugly Incident

Willie was on hand for one of the ugliest incidents in baseball history. On August 22, 1965, the Giants and Dodgers played an important game in a tight pennant race. Giants' pitcher Juan Marichal had been pitching inside all game long—not hitting opposing batters with pitches but brushing them back away from the plate. Eventually, Dodger catcher John Roseboro decided to send a message. Marichal was at the plate, with Sandy Koufax pitching. After one pitch, Roseboro threw the ball back to Koufax, deliberately whizzing it right past Marichal's head.

Marichal, who later said the ball nicked his ear, went wild with anger. He lifted his bat and slammed it down on Roseboro's head, opening a huge, bloody gash. Both benches emptied. Willie ran straight for Roseboro, who was a friend. He took the catcher's head in his hands and tried to calm him down. Many fans and reporters gave Willie credit for single-handedly ending what could have become a terrible brawl. Willie's handling of the situation earned him a new nickname: Peacemaker Mays.

The injuries didn't seem to slow down Willie at the plate. He had one of his best seasons, belting out a career-high fifty-two homers and batting .317. On September 13, he hit the five-hundredth home run of his career, becoming just the fifth player in major-league history to reach that plateau. One at bat later, he cranked out number 501. But even that wasn't enough for Willie. He hit number 502 a few innings later and ended the season with 505.

The Giants were tied for first place with just six games to play, but the Dodgers went on to claim the pennant. San Francisco finished in second place, two games back. The Giants' season was over. But Willie got a consolation prize. Baseball writers voted him the NL MVP for the second time in his career—eleven years after his first award.

Willie's personal life was looking up as well. He was still getting to know Mae Louise Allen. Willie's son, Michael, by then five years old, came to live with him during the off-season. Willie even helped start a side business, an insurance company called the Willie Mays Agency. Willie was thinking of ways to earn a living after baseball. He also started writing an autobiography, with the help of writer Charles Einstein. It was titled *Willie Mays: My Life In and Out of Baseball*.

But baseball was still the focus for Willie. And the eyes of the baseball world were upon him. His 505 career homers were second only to Mel Ott's 511 in NL history. Ruth's record of 714 was starting to seem unlikely. Willie needed more than two hundred home runs to catch Ruth, and he was already thirty-five years old. But it was only a matter of time before he eclipsed Ott.

Early in the 1966 season, it seemed as though Willie was in a hurry to get the record out of the way. He got six home runs in the first two weeks of the season to tie Ott at 511. The media descended on Candlestick Park, eager to cover the historic record breaker. The extra pressure may have played a role in a slump that Willie dropped into. He had only three hits in his next twenty-three at bats. Franks even sat him out a game to give him a rest.

On May 4, Willie, his fans, and the media were still waiting for home run number 512. The Dodgers came to San Francisco for the last series of a home stand. If Willie wanted to enjoy the record with the San Francisco fans, he had to get to work. But he struck out in each of his first two at bats against pitcher Claude Osteen. On Willie's third plate appearance, Osteen threw a changeup (a slow pitch thrown with the same motion as a fastball) over the outside of the plate. Willie took a hard swing and crushed the ball over the right-field fence. With his 512th home run, he had broken Ott's NL record. The stadium erupted as Willie circled the bases. The fans didn't stop cheering when he reached the dugout either. They made him come back out and tip his hat.

Willie continued to move up baseball's all-time home-run list in 1966. He passed Ted Williams (521) and Jimmie Foxx (534). With home run number 535, Willie stood alone at number two behind Babe Ruth.

The 1966 season was great for Willie and good for the Giants. The team competed hard but fell short, finishing second to the Dodgers yet again. Willie batted .288 with thirty-seven home runs.

Willie turned thirty-six early in the 1967 season. He knew he was slowing down. Franks knew it as well, and he rested Willie more than ever. Willie was still an effective player and an All-Star, but his skills were diminishing. In July, he tried to play with a fever and the shakes, but he had to leave the game and spent five days in the hospital. His strength never really returned. He played in just 141 games that year and batted .263 with twenty-two homers. The Giants, meanwhile, once again finished in second place, 10.5 games behind the Cardinals.

This was the new Willie Mays. No longer was he one of baseball's elite players. But that didn't stop him from starting in the All-Star Game. Willie beat out an infield single to lead off the first inning for the National League. He stole second base, advanced to third on a wild pitch, and scored the game's only run on a double-play ball. The National League won 1–0, and Willie was named the game's MVP.

The 1968 season was in many ways similar to that of 1967. Willie played in 148 games, batting .289 with twenty-three homers. That gave him 579 for his career. Ruth's record was out of reach, but the chase for six hundred was alive and well.

In 1969, however, under new manager Clyde King, Willie had his worst statistical year. Willie and King clashed. At one point, teammates even had to keep Willie from throwing a punch at the new manager. Willie's season was further dampened by knee troubles. He played in just 117 games, hitting thirteen homers and batting .283.

 In 1969, Willie bought an eighteen-room home in Atherton, California—a suburb of San Francisco.

That year, Major League Baseball split the two leagues into two divisions each, East and West. After a playoff series, each division winner advanced to a League Championship Series. The Giants had championship hopes that year. They were in first place on September 22. On that day, Willie hit a memorable home run. He had not been a starter in the game against the San Diego

Padres but came in late as a pinch hitter. He hit a two-run homer that gave the Giants a critical victory. If that wasn't enough, the hit was his six-hundredth career home run. Willie had joined Babe Ruth, becoming one of only two players to hit six hundred (though his friend Hank Aaron was already hot on his heels).

## HANK AARON

One of Willie's friends and rivals in baseball was Henry "Hank" Aaron. In many ways, the two stars' careers mirrored each other. Like Willie, Aaron grew up in the segregated South and began his professional career in the Negro Leagues. He made his major-league debut with the Milwaukee Braves in 1954. Like Willie, Aaron had to change cities with his franchise, as the Braves moved to Atlanta in 1966. And also like Willie, Aaron returned home to the city where his career started in his final years, signing with the Brewers in 1975.

Aaron is most famous for breaking Babe Ruth's home-run record. He faced intense racism as he approached the mark. He even admitted to fearing for his life. But still, he hit his record-breaking 715th career home run on April 8, 1974, and went on to total 755 for his career. That record stood until San Francisco's Barry Bonds broke it in 2007.

The Giants weren't able to hold on to first place, however. They finished in second place in the National League West behind the Atlanta Braves.

The 1970 season marked a brief resurgence in Willie's career. At age thirty-nine, he had one of his best seasons in years, highlighted by his three-thousandth career hit. The hit came on July 18 at home against the Montreal Expos. Willie became the ninth man in major-league history to reach the three-thousand-hit mark. (Hank Aaron had reached the milestone just weeks before.) For the season, he batted .291 and slugged twenty-eight home runs, upping his career total to 620. Meanwhile, the Giants finished in third place in the National League West and missed the playoffs.

---

*"I fed off some of the things [Willie] did. I'd read the paper: He got three hits. I said, 'Boy, I ought to be able to get three hits.' But that was competition. There was no resentment, no animosity [hostility].*"

—HANK AARON ON HIS FRIENDLY COMPETITION WITH WILLIE

---

Willie's good numbers in 1970 helped put to rest suggestions by some that he retire. But Willie still faced criticism. By this time, baseball players were fighting for a better deal from team owners. Players did not like the system by which teams owned their rights and determined their pay. A player could only take a team's offer or leave it—and not play at all. Player Curt Flood led the fight for change.

In a book, Flood lambasted Willie for failing to fight for players' rights, as well as for social causes such as civil rights. Willie had often heard this criticism during his career. But Willie was not interested in becoming a celebrity for a cause. He just wanted to play baseball. And Stoneham paid him well to do so. He gave Willie a two-year, $360,000 contract for the next two seasons. Willie would serve both as a player and an informal coach for the Giants. He would work with younger players in addition to his on-the-field duties.

Willie discovered late in his career that he loved the game of golf. Better yet, wealthy executives were willing to pay a lot of money to play golf with a baseball star. Playing golf with executives and their clients became Willie's off-season job.

To begin the 1971 season, Willie picked up right where he left off. He cranked out four homers in the team's first four games. He turned forty that May but still played at a high level. He batted .271 on the season, with eighteen home runs. They were modest numbers by his standards, but pitchers still feared him, as evidenced by his league-leading 112 walks. Better yet, the Giants won their division and earned a trip to the National League Championship Series (NLCS).

The Giants faced the powerful Pittsburgh Pirates in the NLCS. The Pirates had run away with the NL East, while the Giants had scrapped to beat out the Dodgers. The Pirates were rested and prepared. The Giants were dealing with key injuries. They would have to stage a big upset to get Willie back to the World Series. It wasn't to be, however. The Giants won the first game of the series, but that's all they could manage. Willie hit a two-run homer in Game 2, but it wasn't enough. The Pirates won the series three games to one, ending the Giants' season. Willie and his fans had to wonder if it would be the last playoff game of his career.

# Chapter Eight

# The End of an Era

Even though he'd turn forty-one in the spring of 1972, Willie wasn't yet ready to end his baseball career. But first, he had personal matters to attend to. For almost a decade, he'd been dating Mae Allen. She came to Giants games to cheer him on, and the two had grown very close. Willie was willing to give marriage another shot. The two were married on November 29 in Mexico City, Mexico.

Baseball was going through changes as well. Players were demanding more rights and better pay. At the start of the 1972 season, the players briefly went on strike to make their point. They refused to play until owners agreed to some of their demands. As a result, the season started late. Willie's rhythm was thrown off, and he stumbled out of the gate. The Giants weren't winning either. By May 10, they were just 8–16. There were rumors that Willie would be traded. The Giants assured

Willie that the rumors were false. He didn't believe a trade could ever really happen.

On May 11, a reporter called Willie and asked a question that shocked him: How did he feel about being traded to the Mets? That was how Willie first heard the news. The organization he'd been with for more than two decades had traded him to the New York Mets for pitcher Charlie Williams and cash.

Willie had mixed feelings. He was hurt that Stoneham had traded him and that he'd had to hear about it from a reporter. On the other hand, he was headed back to the city he loved. He would be playing for the Mets, who many believed were good enough to win a championship that year.

Willie's return to New York was an emotional affair. And if he wasn't under enough pressure already, his first game would be at home, in Shea Stadium, against none other than the San Francisco Giants.

At the start of the game, the Mets fans gave Willie a huge standing ovation. He walked in his first plate appearance, later coming in to score. Then, with the game tied 4–4 in the bottom of the fifth, Willie came to the plate, wanting to hit a home run. And that's exactly what he did. He hit the ball out on a full count against former teammate Sam McDowell. The crowd erupted as Willie rounded the bases. Willie was home, and he was a New York hero once again.

Willie later described what it was like to circle the bases after the home run: "I get to third [base] and look in the dugout, not in the Mets dugout, in the Giants dugout, and they're all clapping." It was an emotional moment for Willie. He said, "My knees started shaking and I'd never shaken in baseball in my life."

Mae joined Willie in New York. The couple rented an apartment in the city. Willie and the Mets played hard, despite a rash of injuries. In June, Hank Aaron passed Willie on baseball's home-run list, but Willie didn't mind. He knew that Aaron was well on his way to breaking Ruth's hallowed record.

---

*"[Willie] is a hitter all right, and one of the best that ever lived. But this man does it all. He fields, he runs, he studies, he hardly ever makes mistakes. He is a very special person.* 💬

—JOE DIMAGGIO AT WILLIE'S FORTIETH BIRTHDAY PARTY

---

The Mets traveled to San Francisco on July 21 for a series against the Giants. The San Francisco fans gave Willie a big ovation. He came through during the game, hitting a two-run homer in the fifth inning to give the Mets a 3–1 victory. It was home run number 650 of his career. Once again, the Giants fans cheered as though he'd hit it for their team.

Due to injuries, Willie played in just eighty-eight games that season. He batted .250 with eight home runs—all of them with the Mets.

Was it time to retire? Willie seriously considered it. He asked his friend and former manager Herman Franks. Franks told Willie that he could still hit. He thought Willie had one season left in him. So Willie returned to the Mets in 1973, hoping for one last shot at the World Series.

The 1973 season was difficult for Willie. Both of his knees were injured. He needed shots of cortisone, an anti-inflammatory drug, just to play. Later in the season, he broke several ribs when he crashed into an outfield fence. Willie's numbers dipped sharply, but fans still selected him to start in a record twenty-fourth All-Star Game. Willie wasn't the game's hero anymore. Instead, he watched his close friend and former teammate Bobby Bonds lead the National League to victory.

Willie's final season was turning out to be a disappointment in every way. The Mets were in last place, 11.5 games out of first, as late as August 5. But then the team caught fire. They charged up the standings and took over first place with just over a week to play. They went from last to first in just over a month. In Willie's final season, he was headed back to the NLCS. For the year, he played in sixty-six games, batting a career-low .211 with six home runs.

The Mets honored Willie with Willie Mays Night on September 25. They held an hour-long ceremony before the game and showered Willie with gifts. Fans cheered long and loud for their hero. But Willie, still hobbled by injury, would not be playing in the game that night.

Willie stepped up to the microphone to address the fans with tears in his eyes. "In my heart, I'm a sad man," he said. "Just to hear you cheer like this for me and not be able to do anything about it makes me a very sad man." Willie's time as a player was just about up. "This is my farewell," he told the crowd.

But the Mets weren't out of surprises. They shocked the Cincinnati Reds in the NLCS, winning the series three games to two. Willie had just three at bats and one hit in the series. But he celebrated alongside his teammates, knowing he would end his career in the World Series.

The Mets faced the Oakland A's. Once again, they were heavy underdogs. The A's won Game 1, 2–1. Game 2 went into extra innings. In the twelfth inning, Willie came to the plate with runners on first and third. Oakland's Rollie Fingers, one of baseball's all-time great relief pitchers, was on the mound. Willie knew Fingers would throw him a fastball. He was ready when it came. He hit a bouncing ball over Fingers's head and into center field. The hit gave the Giants a 7–6 victory and knotted the series at one game apiece.

The series returned to New York, where Willie mostly watched from the dugout as the Mets won two of three games. They needed to win just one of two remaining games in Oakland to be World Series champions. But they couldn't pull it off. Oakland won the final two games. The Mets' season—and Willie's great career—was over. In the series, Willie batted just seven times, getting two hits. It was a bittersweet ending. The Mets had done more than anyone had expected, but victory had escaped them.

Willie's playing days were over, but the Mets wanted him to remain with the franchise. He would be a part-time coach and a mentor to the team's young players. The job sounded like a great fit for Willie. Baseball was the only career he'd ever had, and this would be a way for him to stay in the game. But Willie was miserable as a coach. He felt powerless on the bench. He later wrote, "It was as if I was in a bad dream trying to walk and something was holding me back. That's how I felt if I sat in the dugout and couldn't contribute."

In time, Willie's duties became more about promoting the team to fans. He stayed on the Mets' payroll, but the job took very little of his time. So Willie took jobs with different companies. They paid him to play golf and eat meals with corporate executives and clients. Just having a baseball star around was good for business. It was hardly satisfying work, so Willie also worked with charities. He created the Say Hey Foundation. This charity raised money to send needy students to college.

---

*"The greatest challenge [of my life was] adjusting to not playing baseball. . . . I had to come out of baseball and come into the business world, not being a college graduate, not being educated to come into the business world the way I should have. And, instead of people doing things for me, I had to do things for myself. That was scary for me."*

—WILLIE MAYS

---

In 1979, Willie had been retired for more than five years. That made him eligible for the Baseball Hall of Fame. His induction was a foregone conclusion. "This country is made up of a great many things," Willie said in his induction speech. "You can grow up to be what you want. I chose baseball, and I loved every minute of it."

 In 1979, the Giants retired Willie's number-24 jersey. No Giant will ever wear Willie's number again.

One of the companies Willie worked with was Bally's, a casino in Atlantic City, New Jersey. Willie had nothing to do with the gambling side of the business, but baseball commissioner Bowie Kuhn was worried. Willie was still on the Mets payroll. Kuhn believed that any association between baseball and gambling was bad news. Such an association might lead to rumors that baseball players fixed games to make money for gamblers. Kuhn took a strong stance. He told Willie that he couldn't work for a big-league team as long as he worked for a gambling organization. The experience left Willie sour. He stopped attending baseball events altogether.

Five years later, new baseball commissioner Peter Ueberroth lifted the ban. Willie returned to baseball. He worked with the Giants in spring training. But it was another influence that really brought his attention back to the game. Willie had become close with teammate Bobby Bonds during his later years on the Giants. Bonds often brought his son Barry to the games. The younger Bonds latched on to Willie, and the two formed a bond. Willie even became Barry's godfather.

Barry followed his father into baseball. He played his first major-league season, as a Pittsburgh Pirate, in 1986. The young Bonds soon made a big impact on the game. In 1990, he was the NL MVP—his first of seven MVP awards. In 1993, he moved to the San Francisco Giants.

Throughout the 1990s and early 2000s, Bonds played at a level that even Willie would have been hard-pressed to match. Willie cheered from the stands as his godson set a new single-season home-run record with seventy-three in 2001. Bonds later said that one of his greatest thrills was passing Willie on baseball's all-time home-run list. Willie was on hand to watch the historic homer, number 661.

---

*"It's his time. I think that every generation has someone like him. When I played, it was me and Aaron. Now it's his time.*"

—WILLIE ON GODSON BARRY BONDS AS BONDS APPROACHED BABE RUTH'S HOME RUN RECORD

---

When Bonds was accused of using steroids (performance-enhancing drugs) in the early 2000s, Willie never criticized his godson. He remained a friend to Barry, even when Bonds had few friends left. In fact, Willie bought his godson a new suit every time he broke another record.

Since his retirement, Willie Mays has tried to stay out of the public spotlight. He and Mae live in California. He makes occasional public appearances at celebrity golf tournaments and All-Star Games. He does his share of charity work, mainly with his Say Hey Foundation. He has continued to pursue his own business ventures. In 2006, he opened a sports bar and restaurant, the Willie Mays Sky Box Lounge, near San Francisco. And, of course, Willie still loves baseball.

## Epilogue

# Willie's Legacy

In the modern game, baseball teams covet the "five-tool player." A five-tool player excels at all facets of the game. He can hit with power. He can hit for a high batting average. He is a smart and speedy base runner. He is a good fielder. And he has a strong throwing arm. Genuine five-tool players are a rarity. Superstars such as Barry Bonds, Ken Griffey Jr., and Alex Rodriguez fit the bill. Inevitably, any five-tool player is compared to Willie Mays.

In many ways, Willie was the ultimate five-tool player. There was nothing he couldn't do. He was a career .302 hitter. He belted out 660 home runs. According to some, he revolutionized the art of the stolen base, leading the league in steals every season from 1956 to 1959 and racking up a total of 338 in his career. And he may have been the greatest defensive center fielder of all time, winning twelve straight Gold Glove Awards from 1957 to 1968.

Willie's numbers were off the charts. Modern baseball fans have a hard time truly appreciating how far ahead of his peers Willie was. His numbers were outstanding. They're even better when one considers the era in which he played. The 1960s and early 1970s were a golden age for pitchers. The mound was higher, giving pitchers greater leverage. The strike zone was bigger, forcing batters to defend more of the plate. And there were no such things as performance-enhancing drugs. Yet Willie managed to produce numbers that would be jaw-dropping even by modern standards.

Willie Mays came into Major League Baseball during a time of tremendous change. Jackie Robinson had broken baseball's color barrier four years before. Robinson will forever remain famous. But his fame springs as much from the fact *that* he played as *how* he played. He was a good player, without question, but not a superstar.

In many ways, Willie Mays was baseball's first African American superstar. His fame came not from the color of his skin but from what he achieved. He was a clubhouse leader, a team captain, and a mentor to younger players of all races. With his trademark enthusiasm and unparalleled raw talent, Willie Mays made his mark on baseball. Many consider him the best player the game has ever seen.

# PERSONAL STATISTICS

**Name:**
William Howard Mays Jr.

**Nickname:**
The Say Hey Kid

**Born:**
May 6, 1931

**Height:**
5' 11"

**Weight:**
180 lbs.

**Batted:**
Right

**Threw:**
Right

**Position:**
Center Field

# REGULAR-SEASON STATISTICS

| Year | Team | G | AVG | HR | RBI | R | SB |
|------|------|-----|------|-----|------|------|-----|
| 1951 | NYG | 121 | .274 | 20 | 68 | 59 | 7 |
| 1952 | NYG | 34 | .236 | 4 | 23 | 17 | 4 |
| 1954 | NYG | 151 | .345 | 41 | 110 | 119 | 8 |
| 1955 | NYG | 152 | .319 | 51 | 127 | 123 | 24 |
| 1956 | NYG | 152 | .296 | 36 | 84 | 101 | 40 |
| 1957 | NYG | 152 | .333 | 35 | 97 | 112 | 38 |
| 1958 | SFG | 152 | .347 | 29 | 96 | 121 | 31 |
| 1959 | SFG | 151 | .313 | 34 | 104 | 125 | 27 |
| 1960 | SFG | 153 | .319 | 29 | 103 | 107 | 25 |
| 1961 | SFG | 154 | .308 | 40 | 123 | 129 | 18 |
| 1962 | SFG | 162 | .304 | 49 | 141 | 130 | 18 |
| 1963 | SFG | 157 | .314 | 38 | 103 | 115 | 8 |
| 1964 | SFG | 157 | .296 | 47 | 111 | 121 | 19 |
| 1965 | SFG | 157 | .317 | 52 | 112 | 118 | 9 |
| 1966 | SFG | 152 | .288 | 37 | 103 | 99 | 5 |
| 1967 | SFG | 141 | .263 | 22 | 70 | 83 | 6 |
| 1968 | SFG | 148 | .289 | 23 | 79 | 84 | 12 |
| 1969 | SFG | 117 | .283 | 13 | 58 | 64 | 6 |
| 1970 | SFG | 139 | .291 | 28 | 83 | 94 | 5 |
| 1971 | SFG | 136 | .271 | 18 | 61 | 82 | 23 |
| 1972 | SFG/NYM | 88 | .250 | 8 | 22 | 35 | 4 |
| 1973 | NYM | 66 | .211 | 6 | 25 | 24 | 1 |
| Totals | | 2,992 | .302 | 660 | 1,903 | 2,062 | 338 |

Key: **G**: games; **AVG**: batting average; **HR**: home runs; **RBI**: runs batted in; **R**: runs; **SB**: stolen bases

# DEFENSIVE STATISTICS (OUTFIELD)

| Year | Team | G | CH | PO | A | E | FLD% |
|------|------|---|----|----|----|----|------|
| 1951 | NYG | 121 | 374 | 353 | 12 | 9 | .976 |
| 1952 | NYG | 34 | 116 | 109 | 6 | 1 | .991 |
| 1954 | NYG | 151 | 468 | 448 | 13 | 7 | .985 |
| 1955 | NYG | 152 | 438 | 407 | 23 | 8 | .982 |
| 1956 | NYG | 152 | 438 | 415 | 14 | 9 | .979 |
| 1957 | NYG | 152 | 445 | 422 | 14 | 9 | .980 |
| 1958 | SFG | 152 | 455 | 429 | 17 | 9 | .980 |
| 1959 | SFG | 151 | 365 | 353 | 6 | 6 | .984 |
| 1960 | SFG | 153 | 412 | 392 | 12 | 8 | .981 |
| 1961 | SFG | 154 | 400 | 385 | 7 | 8 | .980 |
| 1962 | SFG | 162 | 439 | 429 | 6 | 4 | .991 |
| 1963 | SFG | 157 | 412 | 397 | 7 | 8 | .981 |
| 1964 | SFG | 157 | 386 | 370 | 10 | 6 | .984 |
| 1965 | SFG | 157 | 356 | 337 | 13 | 6 | .983 |
| 1966 | SFG | 152 | 385 | 370 | 8 | 7 | .982 |
| 1967 | SFG | 141 | 287 | 277 | 3 | 7 | .976 |
| 1968 | SFG | 148 | 315 | 301 | 7 | 7 | .978 |
| 1969 | SFG | 117 | 208 | 199 | 4 | 5 | .976 |
| 1970 | SFG | 139 | 282 | 269 | 6 | 7 | .975 |
| 1971 | SFG | 136 | 200 | 192 | 2 | 6 | .970 |
| 1972 | SFG/NYM | 88 | 144 | 138 | 3 | 3 | .978 |
| 1973 | NYM | 66 | 106 | 103 | 2 | 1 | .991 |
| Totals | | 2,992 | 7,431 | 7,095 | 195 | 141 | .981 |

Key: G: games; CH: chances; PO: putouts; A: assists; E: errors; FLD%: fielding percentage

# POSTSEASON OFFENSIVE STATISTICS

| Year | Team | G | AVG | HR | RBI | R | SB |
|---|---|---|---|---|---|---|---|
| 1951 | NYG | 6 | .182 | 0 | 1 | 1 | 0 |
| 1954 | NYG | 4 | .286 | 0 | 3 | 4 | 1 |
| 1962 | SFG | 7 | .250 | 0 | 1 | 3 | 1 |
| 1971 | SFG | 4 | .267 | 1 | 3 | 2 | 1 |
| 1973 | NYM | 4 | .300 | 0 | 2 | 2 | 0 |
| CAREER | | 25 | .247 | 1 | 10 | 12 | 3 |

Key: G: games; AVG: batting average; HR: home runs; RBI: runs batted in; R: runs; SB: stolen bases

# GLOSSARY

**amateur:** an athlete who is not paid to play

**autobiography:** a book written about one's own life

**bunt:** to push or tap a baseball lightly with the bat instead of swinging at it

**changeup:** a pitch thrown with the same motion as a fastball but traveling much more slowly

**cortisone:** an anti-inflammatory drug

**curveball:** a pitch that curves in flight

**fastball:** a fast, straight pitch

**minor leagues:** in baseball, teams that serve as training grounds for major-league players. Most minor-league teams are owned by or affiliated with a major-league team.

**pennant:** In baseball, a National League or American League championship. Pennant winners go on to play each other in the World Series.

**pinch hitter:** a player inserted into a baseball game to bat in place of another player

**pop fly:** a high fly ball

**rookie:** a first-year player

**sacrifice fly:** a fly ball that is caught by an outfielder but that allows a runner to score after the catch

**scout:** an employee sent out by a sports team or other organization to look for new talent

**segregation:** the separation of different groups, such as people of different races

**semipro baseball:** a level of baseball below the professional level, where players are paid only small amounts of money

**slump:** a long period in which an athlete performs far below his or her normal level

**strike zone:** the area over home plate through which a baseball must pass to be called a strike

# SOURCES

2–3 Stewart Miller, *The 100 Greatest Days in New York Sports* (New York: Houghton Mifflin, 2006), 69.

5 Mary Kay Linge, *Willie Mays: A Biography* (Westport, CT: Greenwood Press, 2005), 3.

8 Ibid., 4.

8 Donald Honig, *Mays, Mantle, and Snider: A Celebration* (New York: Macmillan, 1987), 99.

9 Linge, *Willie Mays*, 6.

10 Academy of Achievement, "Willie Mays Interview," *Academy of Achievement*, February 19, 1996, http://www.achievement.org/autodoc/page/may0int-4 (November 10, 2009).

11 Willie Mays, *Say Hey: The Autobiography of Willie Mays* (New York: Simon and Schuster, 1988), 24.

14 Linge, *Willie Mays*, 12

17–18 Willie Mays, *My Life In and Out of Baseball, as Told to Charles Einstein* (New York: Dutton, 1966), 28–29.

20 Academy of Achievement, "Willie Mays Interview."

22 Mays, *Say Hey*, 53.

22 Associated Press, "For Mays, All-Star Game Was Stage for His Talent," *New York Times*, July 8, 2007, http://www.nytimes.com/2007/07/08/sports/baseball/08mays.html (October 7, 2009).

22–23 Mays, *Say Hey*, 55.

25 Ibid., 60.

26 Mays, *My Life*, 88–89.

27 Mays, *Say Hey*, 68.

28 Ibid., 72.

29 Linge, *Willie Mays*, 80

32 Ibid., 40.

40 Stewart Miller, *The 100 Greatest Days in New York Sports* (New York: Houghton Mifflin, 2006), 71.

41 Linge, *Willie Mays*, 58.

44 Ibid., 74.

51 Associated Press, "For Mays, All-Star Game Was Stage for His Talent," *New York Times*, July 8, 2007, http://www.nytimes.com/2007/07/08/sports/baseball/08mays.html (October 7, 2009).

51 Linge, *Willie Mays*, 93.

59 Mays, *Say Hey*, 168.

62 Linge, *Willie Mays*, 171.

63 John Shea, "May's Game: Say Hey Kid Had Storybook Career in Midsummer Classic Alone," *San Francisco Chronicle*, July 9, 2007, http://www.sfgate.com/cgi-bin/article.cgi?f=/chronicle/archive/2007/07/09/SPG3BQSE1N1.DTL (November 10, 2009).

70 Mays, *My Life*, 267.

72 Linge, *Willie Mays*, 139.

78 William C. Rhoden, "Aaron and Mays: Closer Than You Think," *New York Times*, July 20, 2008, http://www.nytimes.com/2008/07/20/sports/baseball/20rhoden.html (October 7, 2009).

83 Academy of Achievement, "Willie Mays Interview," *Academy of Achievement*, February 19, 1996, http://www.achievement.org/autodoc/page/may0int-6 (October 7, 2009).

83 Mays, *Say Hey*, 245–46.

85 Ibid., 256.

86   Ibid., 259–60.

87   Academy of Achievement, "Willie Mays Interview," *Academy of Achievement*, February 19, 1996, http://www.achievement.org/autodoc/page/may0int-7 (October 7, 2009).

87   Mays, *Say Hey*, 262.

89   Jack Curry, "Mays Feels Surge of Pride as Chase Nears the End," *New York Times*, August 7, 2007, http://www.nytimes.com/2007/08/07/sports/baseball/07mays.html (October 7, 2009).

# BIBLIOGRAPHY

**Books**

Einstein, Charles. *Willie's Time: Baseball's Golden Age.* Carbondale: Southern Illinois University Press, 2004.

Honig, Donald. *Mays, Mantle, and Snider: A Celebration.* New York: Macmillan, 1987.

Klima, John. *Willie's Boys: The 1948 Birmingham Black Barons, The Last Negro League World Series, and the Making of a Baseball Legend.* New York: Wiley, 2009.

Linge, Mary Kay. *Willie Mays: A Biography.* Westport, CT: Greenwood Press, 2005.

Mays, Willie. *My Life In and Out of Baseball, as Told to Charles Einstein.* New York: Dutton, 1966.

———. *Say Hey: The Autobiography of Willie Mays.* With Lou Sahadi. New York: Simon and Schuster, 1988.

Miller, Stewart. *The 100 Greatest Days in New York Sports*. New York: Houghton Mifflin, 2006.

Shannon, Mike. *Willie Mays: Art in the Outfield*. Tuscaloosa: University of Alabama Press, 2007.

**Articles**

Academy of Achievement, "Willie Mays Interview," *Academy of Achievement*, February 19, 1996, http://www .achievement.org/autodoc/page/may0int-6.

Associated Press, "For Mays, All-Star Game Was Stage for His Talent," *New York Times*, July 8, 2007, http://www. nytimes.com/2007/07/08/sports/baseball/08mays.html.

Rhoden, William C. "Aaron and Mays: Closer Than You Think," *New York Times*, July 20, 2008, http://www .nytimes.com/2008/07/20/sports/baseball/20rhoden .html.

# WEBSITES

Baseball Almanac: Willie Mays

http://www.baseball-almanac.com/players/player.php?p=mayswi01

*Willie's entry at Baseball-almanac.com includes detailed statistics, biographical information, and fast facts.*

Baseball-Reference.com

http://www.baseball-reference.com

*This catalog of baseball history includes box scores from almost every game ever played, career statistics, all-time leader boards, and much more.*

Major League Baseball

http://mlb.com

*The Major League Baseball website includes scores, statistics, standings, a history section, and player profiles from past and present.*

National Baseball Hall of Fame: Willie Mays

http://www.baseballhalloffame.org/hofers/detail.jsp?playerId=118495

*Willie's page at the Hall of Fame includes basic biographical information, a photo gallery, and an image of his Hall of Fame plaque.*

Negro League Baseball

http:www.negroleaguebaseball.com

*This site offers a host of information on the history of the Negro Leagues, including teams and players.*

# INDEX

**105**